From
PUERTO RICO
to
EL BARRIO

Charleston, SC
www.PalmettoPublishing.com

From Puerto Rico to El Barrio
Copyright © 2022 by Eddie Diaz

All rights reserved

No portion of this book may be reproduced, stored in a retrieval system, or transmitted in any form by any means–electronic, mechanical, photocopy, recording, or other–except for brief quotations in printed reviews, without prior permission of the author.

First Edition

Hardcover ISBN: 979-8-88590-994-5
Paperback ISBN: 979-8-88590-969-3

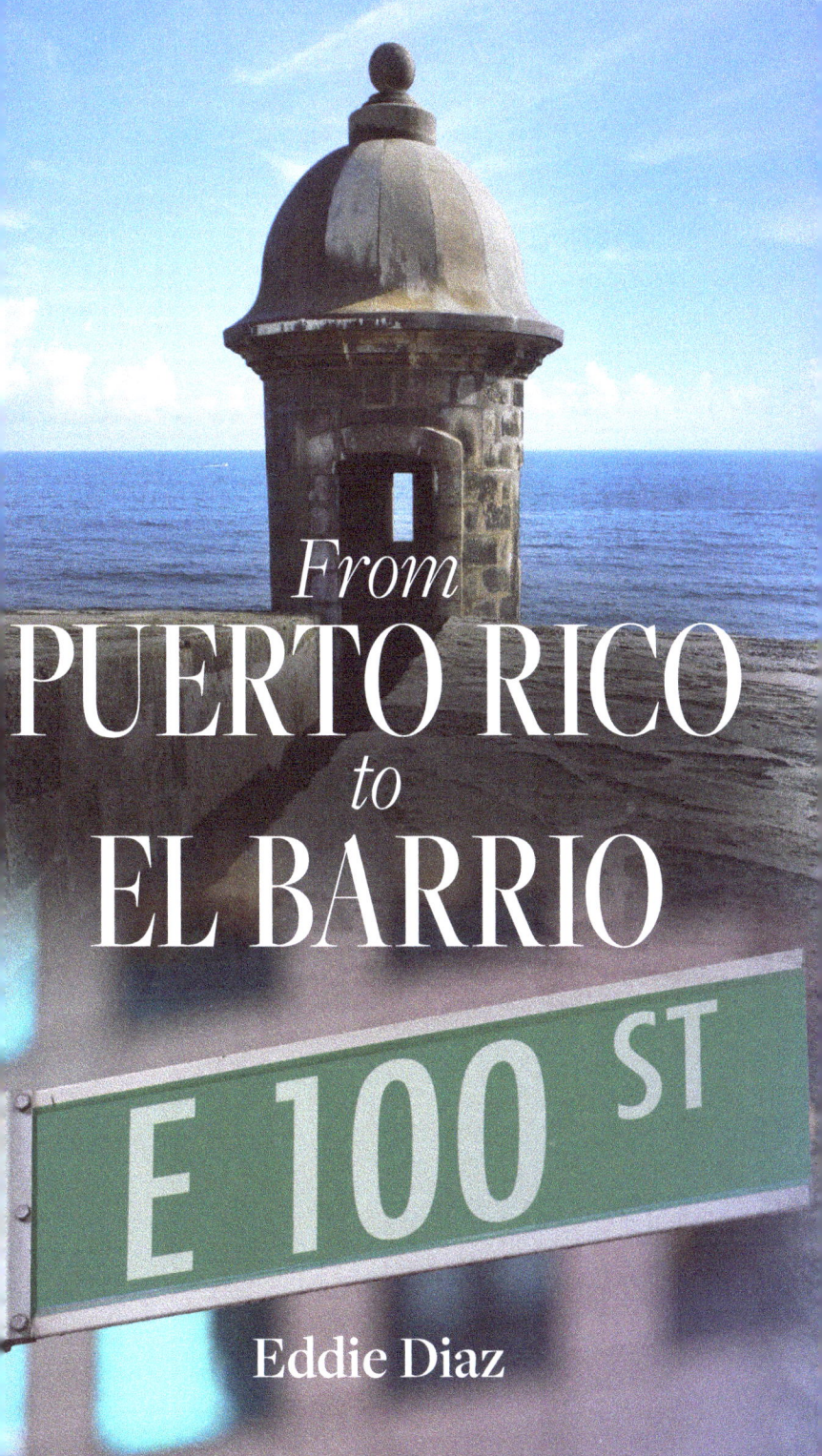

The Three Brothers - Sammy, Kenny & Eddie Diaz

The Diaz Family

The Three Brothers - Eddie, Sammy & Kenny

Eddie's Class Graduation

Sammy in Uniform with brother Kenny

Sammy's Recruit Training Class

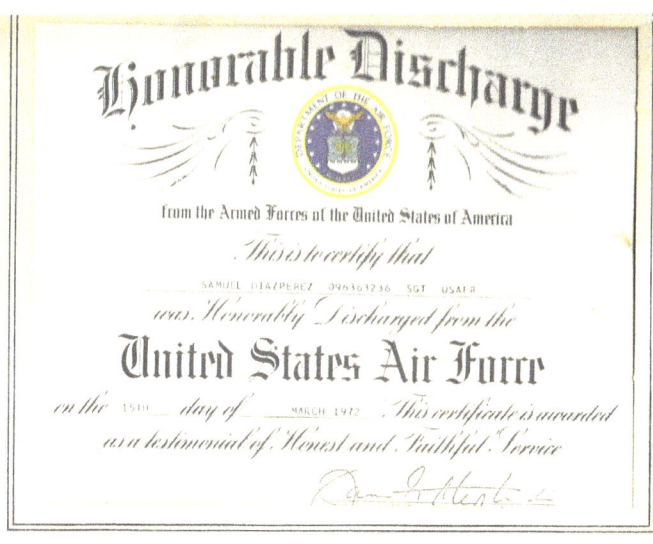

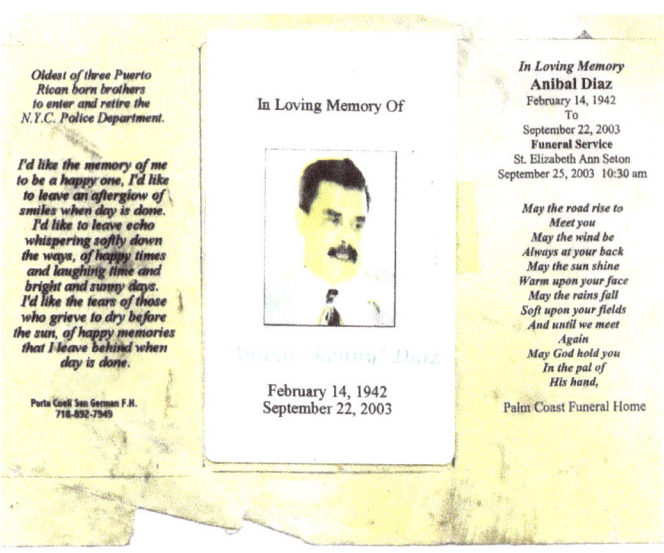

Oldest of three Puerto Rican born brothers to enter and retire the N.Y.C. Police Department.

I'd like the memory of me to be a happy one, I'd like to leave an afterglow of smiles when day is done. I'd like to leave echo whispering softly down the ways, of happy times and laughing time and bright and sunny days. I'd like the tears of those who grieve to dry before the sun, of happy memories that I leave behind when day is done.

Porta Coeli San German F.H.
718-852-7949

In Loving Memory Of

"Kenny" Diaz

February 14, 1942
September 22, 2003

In Loving Memory
Anibal Diaz
February 14, 1942
To
September 22, 2003
Funeral Service
St. Elizabeth Ann Seton
September 25, 2003 10:30 am

May the road rise to
Meet you
May the wind be
Always at your back
May the sun shine
Warm upon your face
May the rains fall
Soft upon your fields
And until we meet
Again
May God hold you
In the pal of
His hand,

Palm Coast Funeral Home

ISRAEL — ANIBAL DIAZ

Eddie at Kenny's Police Graduation and Dad

Members of the Police Martial Arts Club with (center left) Shinan Antonio Perreira, HPCLD, President Mike Nunez, A.C. Anthony V. Bouza, Mr. Herb Miller, Community Affairs, Bronx Boro Office and Officer Joe Sierra, Police Martial Arts Club President.

The Martial Arts Alternative

The exhibition begins with a dazzling and terrifying array of "street" weapons, no guns, all of which can be purchased for less than five dollars in hardware stores, and easily converted into lethal weapons.

How does the police officer defend himself without using his gun or buy time and space to use the gun if necessary?

If he is a member of the Police Martial Arts Club, he or she, knows several quick moves especially designed to disarm and restrain the suspect with a minimum of physical force.

Founded five years ago, the Police Martial Arts Club has 150 members including about 10 women, from federal, state and city law enforcement agencies. The Club's goals are to diminish reliance on weaponry and brute force in the lawful duties; to make the law enforcement person more confident and professional in the performance of his duties; to improve the law enforcement officer's physical fitness; to maximize the health and safety of perpetrator, law enforcement officer and bystander.

Police Officer Joe Sierra, founder and club president first became interested in the martial arts in 1963. He entered the Marine Corps that year where he received additional training. During his full tour in Vietnam and subsequent tours in Korea and Japan, he furthered his knowledge training with soldiers of the Tiger Division, Korean Marines.

Believing that there should be more Hispanic police, Officer Sierra's father, a Mexican revolutionary who fought at Vera Cruz in 1921, insisted that he take the Police exam before leaving the Marine Corps. Accepted by the Police Academy, he left the Marine Corps in 1967. During his nine years in the Police Department he has worked in almost every South Bronx precinct, as well as in Manhattan and in Youth Gang Intelligence.

That same year, 1967, he looked up Shinan (Teacher) Antonio Perreira, whom he had learned about while in the Marines. A Puerto Rican who has studies various martial arts systems in Japan, the Philippines, Australia and New Zealand, Shinan Perreira had developed a program, based on the system used by the Japanese police, specifically for police officers. In addition, he had developed his own form of self-defense tactics which combines elements of judo, karate, aikido and jujitso.

Located on the corner of Third and Tremont Avenues, Shinan Perreira's "dojo" (gymnasium) contains health spa facilities as well as class rooms for martial arts and general physical fitness programs. Founded in 1960, the school has trained more than 13,000 men, women, and children in self-defense tactics.

Here the members of the Police Martial Arts Club take two or three classes per week, learning martial arts and the special police tactics. For example, women are taught how to defend themselves

in MIYAMA RYU JU-JUTSU

GENERAL REQUIREMENTS:

1. Unquestioned moral character and maturity.

2. Continued practice and involvement in Miyama Ryu.

3. Teaching ability.

4. Organizational experience with exhibitions.

5. General promotion of Miyama Ryu.

6. Contribution to the Ryu.

7. TIME-IN-GRADE: Minimum of 5 years since the last promotion. The "Time-in-Grade" requirement may be decreased at the sole discretion of the Shinan, on the basis of Contribution to the Ryu.

ABILITY TO DEMONSTRATE:

SPECIALIZATIONS:
For Example:

a) Ancient Katas

b) Advanced Jodo Katas

c) Miyama Ryu Jo-Jutsu Katas

d) Miyama Ryu Bokkendo Katas

e) Weaponry Katas and Techniques

f) Approved Katas created by the Candidate

g) Approved Katas from other Ryu

h) Any other Kata acceptable to the Shinan and the Board of Examiners.

NOTE: Whatever Katas or techniques are performed for the promotion to Kaiden, they may not be a repeat of those performed for the promotion to Oku-iri, Mokuroku, or Menkyo.

Our mother of five brought us from Puerto Rico to New York on September 28, 1952. She had made a promise to a Saint, she asked him to help her hit a number to bring us to New York. Our father, because there was no work in Puerto Rico, had come ahead to find work in 1951.

As luck would have it my mother hit the number and sure enough, we were on our way to New York. We landed at Idlewild Airport which is now known as Kennedy Airport. I was five maybe six years old. I give my mother a lot of credit lugging five kids to an unknown land just to be united with her husband.

One of our uncles took us in for a while which seemed like an eternity. We would all live in a one room huddled together because there was nowhere else to go.

I remember in those days the boiler used coal and many times having to help my mother shovel coal into the boiler because we had to earn our keep. I still remember my mother's face and arms black with the soot from the coal.

No one had told me that in New York they spoke a different language which was foreign to me. I still remember the fear of not knowing what people were saying to us or about us. Many times, my oldest brother and I were chased all the way home and never really knowing why.

I remember how difficult it was in school not only to learn but to get along with the kids and not knowing what was being said. In those days, because of the cold weather, we wore these stupid looking pilot hats that had fur for the ears. The teacher would tell me something and not knowing what was being said, she would take the hat off and hit me on the head with it to show me that you could not wear hats in class.

I vividly remember because I did not know the area where I was taken to school and told that I was to wait by the brown door after school let out. I would be picked up by my oldest sister or my mother. For some reason I would walk around the block because all the doors in the school looked identical. It seemed like I was always lost. This is probably why I grew up with no sense of direction.

Being Puerto Rican and thrown into 117th Street and First Avenue in Manhattan, which was an all-Italian neighborhood, was probably the most traumatizing experience of my youth. My father when he came to New York had found a furnished room in Brooklyn on Nostrand Avenue. I remember how my brothers and I would take turns visiting him on weekends. It was such a treat to get away from that cramped up guest room and spend time with my father in a pretty brownstone owned by a little Jewish woman. At times I can still smell the coffee that she used to make. Although it was only one room, it seemed such a treat to get away from the crowded room.

One of our happiest moments was when we were told that we were going to move into a bigger apartment, with two bedrooms, kitchen, living room and bathroom, all to ourselves, and also that our father would be reunited with us. We would not have to wait our turn to use the bathroom anymore because the people that owned the apartment had preference when it was used. No more shoveling coal, no more being chased by people, and not knowing why we were being chased. Our father had told us that if we ever had a problem all we had to say was "I live in jeah". It took us many years to realize that what he meant was "I live there". To this day my oldest brother Kenny and I would laugh so much because we found it so funny. But at the time it was very serious. Anyway, a new beginning somewhere other than there.

I remember how on a hot summer day we were going to our new apartment on 100th Street between

First and Second Avenue there must have been a thousand people on the street. The hydrants were full blast and people seemed to be having so much fun. It was like being taken from a passive location to a jungle. My God, what happened! It was like night and day. People all over the fire hydrants being thrown into the water. It was complete chaos. I remember when we were almost arriving to our building someone raised the water of the hydrant and wet us. The confusion that hit us, we were not used to this. All we wanted was to move in. This was a different world. I was not sure if this was going to be a happy place to live in. But the idea of so much room, so different than where we had been exposed to with people around us that spoke the same language made it pretty easy to deal with.

It was here on 100th Street that my mother gave birth to her sixth child, a girl, another one to cramp us up some more. We weren't going to move again; we couldn't afford it. We purchased a Castro Convertible, a small cot, that we could open and close daily and we were on our way. It was on this block that opened up an awareness to my life. This block that had come out in the New York Times as the worst block of the city was a junkie's paradise. This block that had the true hard-core individuals, and also the most respectable and kindest of people I've ever known. How they could live and survive side by side together is beyond my understanding. How they watched out for each other, the faintest of heart, and the true human animal. Guys that did not give a damn if they lived or died and the church goers existing among each other with love and respect and outsiders were not welcomed. This was the block to belong to in the 1950's and 1960's during an era that you had to belong to a gang. The Unknows were from 100th Street, The Conservatives were from First Avenue. In the surrounding area there were so many gangs, The Comanches and The Turbans and who could forget the ongoing wars between The Dragons and The Viceroys and further north The Red Wings.

There were many times when they chased us whenever we went to use the Jefferson Pool. If you wanted to swim you had to take 40 or 50 guys with you. We learned to run fast, but we also learned to fight. Many times, if you had to fight whoever won it was left at that. In some of the many fights, we would tear off the antenna of any car available and that swooshing sound that antenna made, you never seem to forget. The stinging feeling when you got hit with an antenna you also never forget. The best defense was to pick up the cover of a garbage can, that's why there were so many cans without covers. After a while the landlords got smart, and they were chaining the covers with the cans together.

Everyone was a lover at heart during this time, you would see on every street corner group harmonizing and in hallways looking for the best echo that could turn those sounds into such pretty music. We went to dances and sets where the singing groups would entertain while everyone did the grind all the way down if you were good, or just simply grinding against the wall. We used to pay a quarter to get into a set but it was well worth it. For the quarter you got drinks and a chance to meet girls and dance all night amongst the dim red light. This was also the era of the group singers like The Tops and The Marbles.

We played fun games like kicking the can, with kites and follow the leader. Everything just seemed such a joyous occasion even playing with the tops. Some guys would take the point that came with the top and insert a nail so you could break the other guys top in half. With the kites, we would place razor blades in the tail so we could cut the other guy's string. It was such a pleasure as you watched the other guy's kite just fading further and further away and knowing the owner of that kite was also watching it in frustration. In follow the leader, the more dangerous the act, like jumping off the third floor onto a mattress was the most exuberating feeling. We would attach a rope from one building and use it to fly over to the next building. We would take turns. By the time you got home to eat, you were exhausted, and you couldn't wait for tomorrow to do it all over again.

The friends that were made during this era seemed to be loving and lifetime friends. Some dead, others disappeared but they are forever in our memories. Just as there was so much fun, we also needed money, so you had to get a job. We went to White Castle, where you would park your 1957 Chevy and girls on roller skates would take your order. Any convertible car you had could transform you from a nobody to now everyone is your friend. If you look at the era of cars, this was it, the T Birds, the Plymouth with its long wings, the Caddy, the Studebaker, the Chevrolets and Fords and all had to have the skirts and white walls. For $1.00 of gas, you drove all week. As I look back on it, that's how it seemed.

The pleasure of going to the drive-in, a couple in the front and a couple in the back. You needed money so my brothers and I got a job carrying groceries, man this was so cool. For taking peoples groceries home they would pay you a dime, sometimes a quarter anything more than that they became your steady customer, and no one could take their groceries. It was your customer! You knew what time to expect them, and you were there. Saturdays meant all day and at the end of the week you had a lot of quarters. Our mother taught us that everything we made was for the household. But even with that, it seemed like a pleasure to be able to help out. The owner of the supermarket on 101st Street and 2nd Avenue was a female by the name of Mollie (may she rest in peace). She allowed us to hang out and carry her customer's groceries. My older brother Kenny and my younger brother Sam and myself, never did we think that this lady would make such a big impact on our lives. She taught us the value of money and was always screaming at us to do everything right – she seemed to rule with an iron FIST. We never wanted to get her mad. All the workers seemed to be terrified of her and she got every ounce of work out of everyone.

My oldest brother Kenny graduated to packing the groceries and she would pay him at the end of the week. I also graduated to packing the groceries and then Sam started packing the groceries. It seemed like a good feeling to have a part-time job. Kenny then went to become a cashier and a very fast one at that. He then left to go to other supermarkets and becoming an assistant manager at some of those supermarkets. I also became a cashier and finally went to other supermarkets. It seemed that I didn't want to do that for the rest of my life.

Growing up I remember there were happy times and always something to do. Another individual who touched our lives in a very positive way was a tall gentle man with very white hair. He was the minister of a church on 100th Street, the East Harlem Protestant Parish. His name was Norm Eddy and we lived in the same building. I remember how he knocked on our door and spoke to our parents to allow us to attend his church. He spoke fluent Spanish. We had belonged to a different church and had mixed feelings about changing. But slowly we did. At this church, he explained that in the summer they would send kids to summer camp and had a lot of different activities.

Summer came and I remember being told that we were all going to camp but to different camps. My God, we had never been separated from each other especially from our parents. But it was so exciting just thinking about it, getting the suitcase ready, picking up flashlights, under clothes and everything was new! Everything was so exciting until the day came and again mixed feeling about leaving. I was shipped off with my younger brother Sam, Kenny went to what they called The Long Trail. My sister Ginger was sent to Boonton, New Jersey with Mr. & Mrs. Force. My youngest sister Estelle was too young, and my oldest sister was too old to go to camp. So off we went! My experiences at these camps learning how to swim, boating, physical activities, religion, learning to play and pray with other individuals was an everlasting experience that to this day, that I am older feel that it taught me so much about life, about fun, about people. All this was because Reverend Norm Eddie knocked on our door. Going to camp every year was something I looked forward to and summer never came fast enough.

To converse with the Reverend was always and to this day still is very exhilarating. Between him and his beloved wife, Peggy, who passed away, was the guiding light in my path. Peggy Eddie also went on to become a minister in the East Harlem Protestant Parish. Until her dying days she was very active in the East Harlem community, may she always rest in peace.

We as a family went to church every Sunday, religiously. We were able to study the bible in church and discussed and ask questions no one had answers to. We were asked to go on the religious radio channel, and we answered questions from the bible. We were allowed on Sundays, as children to deliver the service to all the congregation. Religion played a major part in our lives. Being good Protestant Christians was something that molded us into the people we have become. We grew up with many children on our block. We learned to respect each other and strived for meaningful values. Most of the kids grew up and bettered themselves. Some married, went to the army or moved away. I feel in my heart that they remember 100th Street with love and admiration for those who made it out of the ghetto. Our Pastors Norm and Peggy have long been gone to be of service to our Lord. We remember them and are thankful for their contribution to society as a whole and to us as a family.

In 1968 my oldest brother, Kenny, and I took the police department exam and we both passed it. My youngest brother, Sam, joined the United States Air Force right after graduating from high school. When he returned home from the service, he applied to the Post Office and worked there for a few years. Sam then took the police department test in 1972 and also passed the exam. We became the first three Puerto Rican brothers to become police officers in New York City. Sam told me he had followed in my footsteps from working in the post office to becoming a police officer. Our parents were very proud of us and spent many nights praying for our safety because we were assigned in very bad precincts.

My first day back in uniform….

I had been in narcotics for two years and my time just expired, and I found myself back in uniform, not wanting to. They told me that if I went to a hazardous precinct I would be back in narcotics in no time. Well, here I am in uniform standing in roll call while the sergeant is calling out the names. I find my mind starting to wonder back to the narcotics office, I'm just walking in and hear the lieutenant shouting at someone in the background and I see all the fellows walking around and a few others typing away at their communications. I'm looking in my box to see if there are any messages and now, I go over to see if there are any communications for me – ah there's one, this is for - just then my name is called by the sergeant and he has to call it again until my mind comes back to where I'm at, in uniform.

The sergeant says you're one of the new men, you got post 69. Right face, forward march says the sergeant. I got my baton in the right hand and I'm walking out of the precinct but I just don't know which way to turn to get my post. I asked another uniform man which way to my post and he says "what do I know it's my first day here I came from the 6th District Narcotics". I finally get instructions and I'm on my way and I feel so funny because everyone seems to be looking at me for some reason. Let me check my shoes are shined, my patch is on my right side of my wide stripes and everything is all right, it's just my imagination. I started to walk my beat and I find myself starting to wander again back to the office. This communication looks all right but will have Gene look at it and see if… A lady called out "Officer that man just stole my pocketbook", I looked, and the lady is pointing her finger and I see a man running away. I'm stunned and I start to give chase, for some reason he seems to be running faster than me. I know what it is, I am out of shape due to those years in the office taken effect with this pain on my side. I can't catch up to this guy and had to stop to catch my breath and started to walk back to the lady and she's still in tears. I tried to console her, and it doesn't seem to be doing any good – do I need this! I tried to tell her to come with me to the station to make a complaint and she starts to argue what good it's going to do and she refuses to do so and walks away. So, if she does not want to make a complaint, I can't force her.

I finally got to my post and feel everybody staring at me, it is probably my imagination again. I do not know but I can't do much of this walking so, I'll walk around to see what store looks good so I can go in and have a smoke and talk with the store owner. Ah, that store looks pretty good, as I'm walking, I see a sector car a block away coming from the opposite direction he goes by and makes a U-turn on the corner and pulls up to me and it's the Sergeant. I salute and he says "I'll give you a scratch", (A scratch in Cop language is when the Sergeant signs his name on the book to show that he observed you on your post), so I gave him my book and he makes a note. He does this and drives away. I continue walking towards the store and then another sector car pulls up behind me and the recorder asks, "Are you the man on post?" and I said Yeah, he says you got a psycho at the hospital, and I say to myself "Oh Shit". I get in and he drives me to the hospital and there is a guy that looks like if he gets out of his handcuffs, he will kill anyone that is in a blue uniform. Finally, the doctor admits him and I am going to call for a 10-85 (for assistance). I said to myself, never mind I can get lost for the rest of the tour, might as well they will never know I'm finished. I see a patrol coming to me and he says, "you got the psycho" and I said that he was just admitted. He said the Lieutenant told him to relieve me and told me there is a D.O.A. (Dead on Arrival) and wants me to guard it and for him to relieve me. Oh no, it can't be, I said, and he says yep. Oh, those beautiful years in Narcotics! So, I finally get to the house of the D.O.A and I can smell the odor from the hallway, I put my fingers to my nose, and I start to walk up the stairs to the fifth floor. I got upstairs and the Sergeant is still there and he says "You got this" and walks away. I stand there and a uniform police officer gave me all the information and leaves. I walked around the apartment to make sure everything was all right and the windows open for ventilation. WOW, what a smell! I looked at the body and said to myself, did I just see him move and I stared at the body to make sure, no, it's my mind again. I was standing in the hallway and my mind starts to wander to the time we hit the warrants, the times up in the warrant's office applying for warrants, the times we waited for the undercover to finally get there and I subconsciously start to smile and I catch myself and I say "Damn what am I doing here, can it really be?" and shake my head and damn right it is. Just then the Medical Examiner and the ambulance driver come up the stairs and pronounces him dead and then take the body away just in time since I have twenty minutes to get back to the precinct. I finally made it to the locker room to change and say I made it, what a day.

There are times in our lives when we find ourselves thinking and we say how we would react during certain circumstances, but no one knows that this is not true more than a Police Officer because he has been through so many different unbelievable situations and knows that each one, he had to handle in a different manner. I personally can think of a few incidents that to this day I do not know how I would react if the same events were to reoccur. Certain things are done in such an impulse that one does not have time to think, just react and hope that it turns out for the best. Again, I repeat a Police Officer is more prone to react much more than anyone else.

Looking back through my years as a police officer, I find myself daydreaming about certain events that had occurred to me and I sometimes say "Wow, how in the world did I get out of that". I can think back as far as my police academy days, how I was told and constantly reminded as to how I should react to certain incidents. But it was not until I was actually in the street that I found out that the Academy was only theory. When I first came out of Academy, I said to myself "Now I am a Police Officer and now I'm ready", but was I surprised. I was so disgusted and ashamed that I at first said NO, I know this is not for me. I thank whatever it was that pushed me forward because I know that I have come a long way and certain events as an officer that I experienced shaped me into the person that I am today.

So much for the Rap and I will get on with a few of my experiences. My last day at the academy, I remember all the guys sitting around waiting to find out which precincts they were going to be assigned to. Everyone was laughing as each name and precinct was called. Little remarks were being exchanged for each precinct. Hey Jack, you got twenty-three, I live there, you can come up to my house when you get a coffee break. With this there was laughter but still I could feel a certain nervousness in my stomach and as I looked around, I felt that I wasn't the only one with this feeling and maybe this was the reason why I also felt a little joy and a feeling of adventure at the same time. I will tell you that at that moment I felt so many mixed emotions that I don't think I can explain my feeling and be honest about it. As names and precincts were read out, I started wondering why my name and precinct had not been called. I started to feel a certain nervousness and tenseness within myself because I knew that it would not be long. The coldness that I started feeling was a feeling that I do not think I had ever experienced before. When my name was finally called, I froze. Not because my name had been called but because the Sergeant had said the 41st Precinct. This precinct has been on my mind since the beginning of the academy. All the Sergeant ever spoke of was the 41st Precinct. Any example that was given through the lectures was the 41st Precinct – the 41st Precinct this, the 41st

Precinct that. I knew the reputation of this precinct like I knew the back of my hand.

All that was supposed to live in the 41st Precinct were Indians, which was the reason as to why it was called Fort Apache. Ask any Police Officer about Fort Apache and you will see, like I saw when I was a rookie, a smile from ear to ear with the remark "I'll quit before they send me there". Again, mixed emotions started flowing through me. I started to think good thoughts like that is good because it's only a two-minute ride from my house and I could be there in no time. But this did not help, I started to feel scared again and now I started to think Damn is it worth it or should I quit before I get started. Something within myself started to talk to me and it said, man you never quit before you started something, why now. I answered back man this is different, I am going to the 41st Precinct this is entirely different you know what the Sergeant has said about this precinct. If they had a gadget to measure scarceness, I think it would have broken it had they strapped it to me. Suddenly, a name was called and I started to feel a certain reassurance now. The name was Big George. My heart started to slow down and then I felt a sense of confidence. Big George was also going to the 41st Precinct. Big George was a guy that stood 6'6" and while in the Army was a boxer. He had 40 fights and won 40 fights, undefeated. So, I guess I do not have to explain as to why I felt the gust of confidence all of a sudden. A few more names were called, and Fort Apache now felt a little better, I was not going to be thrown into the 41st Precinct all by myself.

The last day of the Academy was a Friday and through that weekend all I thought about was that come Monday I would be in the 41st Precinct. I even went to the extent on Saturday to go by the to the 41st Precinct and find out what it was about. I rode around the area and I told myself it doesn't really look that bad and the people looked friendly. Monday came and I woke up around 6:00 am because I was due in at 8:00 am, I put on my uniform at home and started on my way to the precinct. I arrived and all the Policer Officer were conversing in their own little groups. None of the fellows from the academy were there and I started to think if something was wrong. Had everyone been transferred at the last minute without me knowing it. A few minutes of heavy thoughts and finally one of the guys came in, a few minutes later Big George entered and then the rest of the guys arrived.

For a few minutes, all one could hear was the echoes from all the conversations at the same time. A Sergeant entered and all he said was "Fall in". Everyone stopped their conversations and lined up for roll call. As each name was called a post was assigned to them. My name was called and post Forty-eight was assigned to me. I asked around to find out which streets did the post cover, and a small book was handed to me by the

Sergeant. The book explained every post and which streets every post covered. This was beautiful but I still did not know where the streets were because I was not familiar with the neighborhood. I said what do I do now and finally one of the fellows from a radio car approached me and he volunteered to drop me off at the post. I thanked him and he reassured me not to worry about anything that they were covering the post on car, and I would see them quite often.

As I walked my post, all I thought about was that if anything happened, I would be able to handle it. I wondered whether I would be able to react in the proper manner. All the thoughts that raced through my mind while on post were so many that I do not think I would have enough space on this page because there were too many. As I walked, I felt that everyone was looking at me and I wondered whether they had good thoughts or bad thoughts of me being there. The day went by pretty quick, and it was good that nothing had happened. I kept looking at my watch and I had 15 minutes left of my tour. Just then as I was standing on Southern Blvd and Wilkens Avenue, I saw that another rookie had the post directly across the street from me. He waved and I waved back. He came over to my post and we started conversing about how easy the day had gone. I looked across to an adjoining post and I observed that there was a group of about 12 guys, and they were bending over in a fashion of that when one is playing dice. I turned and asked the rookie if he thought it was wise to go over and break up the game. He said that it was not our post and we had ten minutes left to end the workday. Just then shots rang out and they came from the crowd. Before we could think, we both started to run towards the crowd that was in the process of dispersing. After a little unplanned strategy on our part, we were able to catch up to seven of them. We had them against a car and now the problem was what to do with them. With guns cocked to their heads they were quiet and very cooperative in standing still. A voice on the other end said what is up and I replied that we needed help. He asked where and I replied Southern and Wilkens. He said on the way and hung up. As I started to run back to where I left the rookie, I heard sirens coming from every direction. Before I got back to the crowd, which was only half a block away, there were already about ten radio cars. One of the officers asked who had called the thirteen and I not knowing what a thirteen was said I did not know. Later I found out that a thirteen is the code when a Police Officer needs assistance. Thank God, that it took that incident for me to learn what a thirteen was because after that incident I've had to use it numerous times.

After that event on Wilkens Avenue, I found myself picturing the event as to how it had happened so suddenly, and I started to congratulate myself on the fact that it was the first day and we had engaged it on impulse alone. I started thinking as to how I would have handled it had I been alone. One never knows how you would react under certain circumstances. Some events a Police Office reacts on impulse alone.

The following day I was assigned to Special Post 6, it was call Special Post, as I found out, because it was a whore post. It was around the corner from the police station. The only problem I had up to around three o'clock in the afternoon was the congestion of traffic under the Westchester Avenue L. The aggravation involved in directing traffic under the L with all the double-parked cars in the way was a hectic experience. The buses for some reason or another were scheduled right behind one another, and this didn't seem to help either. So, between the heat of 90-degree weather, the doubled parked cars, the buses running one after the other, how can one not become frustrated, even if he is a COP.

At around 3:30 pm I noticed that there were people suddenly hanging around, there were small groups of four and five all over the avenue. As I approached the first group to find out what was going on, I noticed that as I approached, they all dispersed and walked away in different directions. I asked myself what the hell is going on and I noticed myself on the guard for something that I felt was about to happen which never did. I then started to walk over the second group, and they also dispersed in different directions and again I was confused and trying to understand the behavior of these people. At 3:40 pm I observed a Police Radio Car on the corner of Simpson Street and as I walked over, I saw the Sergeant. He made a gesture with his hand to come over and he asked me for my memo book to give me a scratch. He signed his name and gave me my book and said keep the whores moving. I told him I was new on the job, and I didn't know what was required on the post. After he explained that these girls were on junk and that they were prostitutes I then realized why they all moved away when I approached.

All the way home I kept asking myself as to why all this was happening right around the corner from the precinct, and nothing had been done about it. If anything, one can easily understand something of the sort happening but damn not right around the corner from so many Police Officers. It did not make any sense. The more I thought about it the more frustrated I became. So, I just pushed it to the side and from that moment on I decided that I would try not to take the job home like so many people do and eventually it throws the family life off base.

The next day it was still on my mind going to work. I came into the station house and went straight to a wall where the roll call was kept, and I noticed that my name was on the roll call for Special Post 6. I did not know if I should have been glad or what, but while going up the stairs to my locker to change into uniform, I stopped an old timer on the stairs and asked him about the post. He said that it had been like that ever since he could remember, and that the reason he thought was that there was a hotel right around the corner, and they had access to it in some form or other. I asked him if that was the case then why had no one closed the hotel. He replied either they don't have enough reason to close it or somebody is getting money somewhere along the line. Being naïve about the second reason I figured the first one had to be the right reason. On post again the traffic was unbelievable. How the hell can there be so much confusion?

Everything leading to the present, can and has to be looked upon with mixed emotions. Our beautiful experiences and our sorrowful experiences as a family that we have shared will be with us until our dying days. Times when we will sit down or lie down, either together or by ourselves and we will say, Gee… Why? And come up with no conclusion, except for the reality that it happened. As a family we have been and should continue being one of strength and sincerity to one another. We cannot forget each other's problems, each other's loneliness, and each other's needs.

With unity there is strength, without it we will crumble. We cannot allow anyone of us to crumble. Nothing and no one should allow this to happen. We must maintain our love and our respect to one another. We must maintain goals to move forward as a whole, and not as little fragments or pieces diverted in different directions because in this way there is no strength. There is no way that we can avoid future sorrows. But there is a way to confront any future sorrows and that is by being together and comforting one another when our time of need is at hand.

I would like to take this opportunity to thank each one of you in the manner in which you all conducted yourselves through this ordeal. You may have broken down many times when you were by yourselves, which in a case as ours is very normal. But, in the eyes of everyone, one could see the envy as to even the last moment we stuck together. People will continue to try to hurt us, but we will continue to show our strength through our unity.

I have dedicated my life to Ju-Jutsu since the age of 24 when I went to see a class in progress and asked the instructor if I could have a class for free and he said NO and we are not monkeys that you can see for free. I have met instructors that have been doing the same thing as myself. Also met many students which I still keep in touched with. Today I hold the title and certificate of Shihan. Shihan is the title for expert, master and Senior Instructor. A Shihan has command of the required material and can apply the knowledge to instruct and lead. I have made Shihan which means I completed all the required belts and techniques.

As I write these few lines, I feel the presence of something guiding my hand in expressing myself. Maybe it's my inner conscience or maybe it's something that I have no understanding for, but whatever it is, it says GOD BLESS YOU.

www.ingramcontent.com/pod-product-compliance
Lightning Source LLC
LaVergne TN
LVHW051041070526
838201LV00067B/4884